INVASIVE
SPECIES

Invasive Insects and Diseases

Kaitlyn Duling

Cavendish
Square

New York

Published in 2017 by Cavendish Square Publishing, LLC
243 5th Avenue, Suite 136, New York, NY 10016

Library of Congress Cataloging-in-Publication Data
Names: Duling, Kaitlyn, author.
Title: Invasive insects and diseases / Kaitlyn Duling.
Description: New York : Cavendish Square Publishing, [2016] | Series: Invasive species | Includes index. | Description based on print version record and CIP data provided by publisher; resource not viewed.
Identifiers: LCCN 2016000171 (print) | LCCN 2015049737 (ebook) |
ISBN 9781502618450 (ebook) | ISBN 9781502618405 (library bound)
Subjects: LCSH: Introduced organisms—Juvenile literature. | Introduced insects—Juvenile literature.
Classification: LCC QH353 (print) | LCC QH353 .D85 2016 (ebook) | DDC 578.6/2--dc23
LC record available at http://lccn.loc.gov/2016000171

Editorial Director: David McNamara
Editor: Renni Johnson
Copy Editor: Nathan Heidelberger
Art Director: Jeffrey Talbot
Designer: Alan Sliwinski
Senior Production Manager: Jennifer Ryder-Talbot
Photo Research: J8 Media

The photographs in this book are used by permission and through the courtesy of: The photographs in this book are used by permission and through the courtesy of: Alin Brotea/Shutterstock.com, cover wrap, 1; Jim Wilkes/Toronto Star via Getty Images, 4; sjgh/Shutterstock.com, 6; Top Photo Corporation/Thinkstock.com (l), Michael Smith/USDA (r), 7; Jasemin90/Shutterstock.com, 6-7 (and used throughout the book); grass-lifeisgood/Moment Open/Getty Images, 10; James H Robinson/Oxford Scientific/Getty Images, 12; Scott Camazine /Science Source, 14; Inga Spence/Science Source, 16; Kittie and Minnie/Shutterstock.com, 18-19; Mary Evans Picture Library/AGE Fotostock, 20; Maciej Noskowski/iStockphoto.com, 23; James Gathany, CDC/File:CDC-Gathany-Aedes-albopictus-1.jpg/Wikimedia Commons, 24; USDA, 30; sl_photo/Shutterstock.com, 30-31 (and used throughout the book); Photo Researchers/Getty Images, 33; Martin Harvey/Gallo Images/Getty Images; 34; Michael Palmer/File:Honey bee on flower with pollen collected on rear leg.jpg/Wikimedia Commons; 37; Willie Anderson/NY Daily News Archive via Getty Images, 38; Cultura RM/Kevin Kozicki/Getty Images, 40; Lucky Team Studio/Shutterstock.com, 42.

Printed in the United States of America

Invasive Insects and Diseases

An Asian longhorned beetle shows off its famous white spots and long antennae. The dime-sized holes in the tree are homes for ALB eggs and larvae.

Invasion of the Tree Snatchers

★

There are aliens among us. Over the last ten years, blue-footed aliens have invaded the United States. Yes, these aliens have turned up along the East Coast, and humans are just starting to learn how to combat their spread. These aliens are small, with black and white spots and long, striped **antennae.** They have bright blue feet and tiny, strong mouths. However, you probably wouldn't notice them. They live deep inside the trees around us, hiding. These creatures are Asian longhorned beetles, or ALBs. They first arrived in the United States nearly thirty years ago. Now, they continue to spread, slowly taking over cities and forests all along the coast and into the Midwest.

AN INVASION UNFOLDS

Toronto, CA Worcester, MA

Chicago, IL

New York, NY and
Jersey City, NJ

Invasive Insects and Diseases

Before an invasion, trees appear healthy, strong, and beautiful.

This red maple has been filled with beetles that bore and tunnel their way through.

A forest in China was planted with American poplar trees. This tree is not native to China. The Asian longhorned beetles loved their new trees and laid eggs into the bark. The ruined trees were cut down and chipped. Then they were turned into shipping containers.

Shipping containers arrive in Brooklyn Harbor in New York, New York. First **infestation** found in 1996.

Chicago, Illinois: ALB infestation found in 1998.

Worcester, Massachusettes: ALB infestation found in 2008. People here are working to get rid of the beetles by cutting down trees.

"Aliens" like the Asian longhorned beetle are also known by another name—invasive insects. Invasive creatures are species that travel to a new place. Their new home might be totally different from where they started! They might not be welcome in the new place, either. Biologists often refer to these traveling bugs as "invaders."

Many of these invaders cause problems when they move into a new country or continent. Harmful insects may destroy plants or hurt the insects and animals already living there. Others can be helpful, like those that control **overpopulation.** When too many species live in an area, there are not enough resources for all the plants and animals to survive. If a forest has too many earthworms, other insects or lizards introduced to the **habitat** could eat the earthworms to help with the problem. Whether they help or hurt, each alien has its own unique journey and story.

How Could This Happen?

Nonnative insects like the ALB are considered invasive when their new home has no natural enemies in it. An enemy could limit the nonnative insects' numbers and growth. Without rivals, insects will overrun an area!

When they are able to dig into yummy poplar trees, Asian longhorned beetles quickly make homes and reproduce. Then they begin to spread through the forest. Within a matter of months or years, the trees are filled with holes. Eventually, they may weaken, rot, and die. The beetles will travel far and wide to find fresh trees. Left unchecked, the species's spread will continue as long as there are trees to chew.

An insect that survives the trip from one country to another could find itself in the perfect place to live and lay eggs. The American hardwood forests are just right for the ALBs. Some unlucky bugs may find that their new home is not a welcome place. They might not have the **adaptations** needed to survive. The temperature could be too cold or too hot. Or they may not be ready to fight off the natural enemies found there. The invasive bug may meet bigger, stronger bugs, birds, and animals that like to feast on them.

When insects cross borders, it really is "survival of the fittest." From tiny Asian tiger mosquitos to huge gypsy moths, invasive insects are a problem all over the globe. As we will see, these aliens can be especially harmful to certain plants, animals, other insects, and even humans!

A group of red ants feast on their prey!

The Ants Have Landed

very creature on Earth needs a place to live and thrive. These places are called habitats. A habitat is made up of all living and non-living **organisms** within a space. This includes things like plants, animals, humans, and even germs. A habitat also includes other parts of an area, like weather.

Think about the habitat you live in. What plants and animals live there? How would you describe it? All habitats also have their own delicate web of **predators** and **prey**. When a new animal or plant moves into that area, even if it is a tiny insect, it changes the habitat, and the result is not always good.

A ladybug, or ladybird beetle, dives into a meal of aphids.

A predator is an animal that needs to eat other animals in order to survive. It might be a hunter, like a lion who eats zebras in the wild. A spider waiting for flies in her web is also a predator. The food predators catch is called prey. When it comes to invasive bugs, trees and plants aren't the only ones that need to worry. An insect that is brought to a new habitat can cause a serious problem in the **food chain**. A food chain is the link of predators and prey. This link keeps the number of animals in balance. For example, the number of aphids in a garden can be controlled by ladybugs. Ladybugs like to feed on the aphids. In turn, spiders and beetles eat the ladybugs. Each of the insects keeps the number of other bugs in check.

Spreading Like Wildfire

One of the best examples of an upset habitat is the story of the red imported fire ant, or RIFA. Native to South America, these ants and their fierce bites were first brought to the United States in the 1930s. Experts believe they entered the country in Mobile, Alabama. After they worked their way into the United States, these ants became a big issue for humans. People didn't like their nasty bites, and the ants caused chaos in their new habitat. RIFAs live in huge groups. There can be one hundred thousand to five hundred thousand ants filling a mound at any one time. The mounds are found in parks, on roadsides, and in other open areas. Once they have moved in, it is very hard to get rid of these ants. Due to their large size, RIFA mounds tend to cause problems wherever they go.

And they have been moving farther and farther north for the past eighty years.

New species compete with other insects in their habitats. Red imported fire ants compete with native ants. Ants are considered native to the United States if they have always lived there, like the carpenter ant. There is even one native species called the "crazy ant." The RIFA takes up space and food from carpenters,

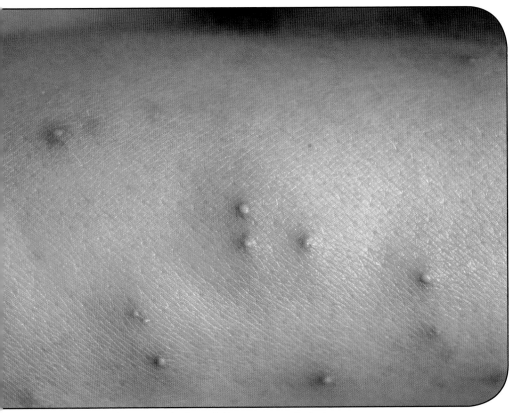

RIFA bites leave a trail of painful bumps on unlucky humans.

crazy ants, and others. The new species often forces the other ants to find somewhere else to live. When native ants leave, the habitat and food chain are forced to change. In addition to impacting their fellow ants, RIFAs have affected larger animal species. There have been many reports of RIFAs biting and killing small birds, rodents, and lizards. They have even killed newborn cattle and deer.

It may take years to find out the true impacts of this new bug. Luckily, it already looks like some animals are adapting to the ant. Scientists have seen young lizards fighting off the ants even better than their parents. And the youngest lizards have longer hind legs. The longer legs help them kick the RIFAs off and away from their bodies. They have adapted to fight their new invasive enemy. We can expect more changes like these as long as species continue to travel.

A Plague on Forests

In the future, we can expect both short-term and long-term effects from alien insects. One of the worst additions to North American forests is the gypsy moth. These were first brought to Massachusetts over one

TREES GET SICK, TOO

Reddish sap oozes from an oak tree afflicted with sudden oak death.

Bugs aren't the only ones changing our forests. When you know what to look for, it is easy to spot the signs of invasive diseases in trees, shrubs, and other plants. A sickness called sudden oak death has been tearing through California and Oregon since 1995. Caused by a fungus that scientists recently discovered, SOD causes leaves to suddenly turn brown. Cankers can form, and ooze bleeds from the trees' bark! Biologists are still working to stop the spread of SOD.

Another invasive disease is caused by a special fungus called blue stain, carried by bark beetles. The sticky spores of the fungus form inside trees. This makes it hard for the trees to collect water, and eventually they die. A large "blue stain" can be found in the cross-sections of infected trees. The result isn't all bad, though—the disease does not affect the strength of the wood at all. Many people like to buy furniture, flooring, and other products made of blue-stained wood.

hundred years ago. Since then, these moths have torn through acres of forest. They fly farther every year and eat leaves as they go. When gypsy moths first move into an area, the short-term effects are clear. Suddenly, trees and plants lose all their leaves. This is called **defoliation.** You can see the moths' work as you walk through the forest.

Though the gypsy moth has been in North America for over a hundred years, we have yet to see what all of its long-term effects will be. We do know that when trees infested with the moth die, sometimes other tree species grow in their place. The moths may not eat the new trees, which could save the forest, but this is not guaranteed. Chemicals have been sprayed on trees to kill the moths, which troubles some scientists. We do not yet know the full effects of these chemicals on other plants, animals, or the water supply. Humans will have to wait and see how the gypsy moth will change the forests across the United States.

Invaders to North America

West Nile virus
Formosan subterranean
  termite
Brown marmorated stink bug
Ladybird beetle
Asian longhorned beetle
Asian tiger mosquito
Earthworms
European honeybee
Boll weevil
Red imported fire ant
Gypsy moth
Medfly
Sudden oak death

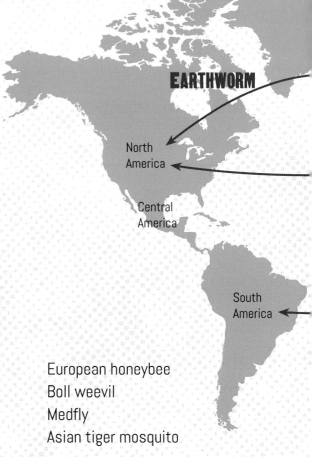

EARTHWORM

North
America

Central
America

South
America

Central America

Ladybird beetle
Formosan subterranean
  termite
European honeybee
Red imported fire ant
Blue stain
Asian tiger mosquito

European honeybee
Boll weevil
Medfly
Asian tiger mosquito

Europe

West Nile virus
Ladybird beetle
Asian longhorned beetle
Asian tiger mosquito
Sudden oak death
Blue Stain

South America

Ladybird beetle
Formosan subterranean
  termite

BROWN MARMORATED STINK BUG

Europe

Asia

Middle East

Africa

LADYBIRD BEETLE

Australia

Africa
Formosan subterranean
 termite
Ladybird beetle
Asian tiger mosquito

Middle East
Ladybird beetle
Asian tiger mosquito

Asia
West Nile virus
Formosan subterranean
 termite
Red imported fire ant

Australia
Earthworms
Red imported fire ant
Medfly

Like UFOs, "alien" insects can cause chaos wherever they invade.

3 You're Invited

★

It might seem like invasive insects drop into new areas like Martians on UFOs. The truth is, however, that people often cause these invasions. Bugs do not simply decide to travel. They do not plan fun vacations. Insects have been brought to new areas through containers of goods. They have traveled on fruits. Even tourists have brought them! Whether they mean to or not, people do bring insects from one country to another. They may even move bugs to a new continent. Insects have often become invasive by accident, especially after the start of **global trade**. Every day, goods travel to and from cities across the world. Insects often hitch a ride. Many times, they arrive by boat. These creatures, once settled in a new place, can ruin crops and livestock. They can also ruin property and spread diseases.

What in the World?

Do you know where your shirt, shoes, or pencils were made? We buy our food, clothes, and more at stores in our cities and towns. However, most of the things we buy have traveled across the globe! All day and all night, ships and planes are traveling. They are moving furniture, toys, cell phones, and more. It is very easy for insects to join these trips. Some live in wooden pallets. Others ride over in flowers or food. This is why we have to watch our trade! There are many policies in place to keep us safe from traveler bugs, but as we'll see, they don't always work. Once they take off, these bugs find homes in our forests and towns. Before we know it, an "invasion" has begun.

One of the first bugs brought into the United States is now one of the most common. You see them while digging in the garden or during a rainstorm. You might even use them to catch fish! Earthworms were probably brought here by some of the first settlers, who came on boats. Their boats were filled with dirt to keep them balanced, and that dirt was filled with worms.

Many different kinds of worms traveled from Europe and Asia. Today, the worms you see in the soil are probably aliens who moved in long ago. With all that wiggling, they help keep our soil rich and fresh. Some scientists do worry about competition between the worms and other species. Others have found issues with

All kinds of goods (and stowaway bugs) travel across the globe in shipping containers just like these.

worms taking over the forest floor. We will have to wait and see how they change our soil in the years ahead.

Not What We Ordered

One of the most famous diseases of our time is the West Nile virus. This disease is usually carried by mosquitos. West Nile can give you a fever and rash.

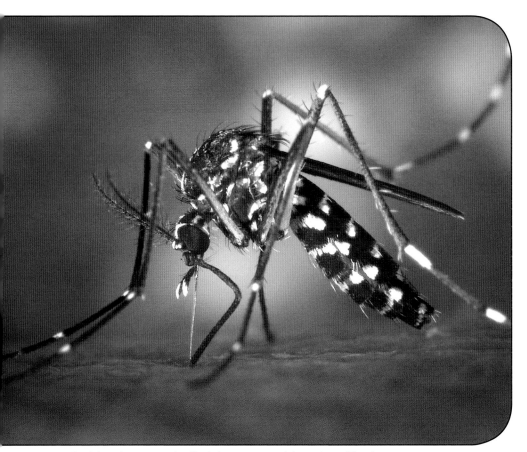

An Asian tiger mosquito finds human prey. Mosquitoes like these can carry West Nile virus.

It can sometimes be deadly! In this case, an invasive disease and an invasive insect are connected. One mosquito that carries West Nile is the Asian tiger mosquito. It is also known to carry other diseases.

As the name suggests, the Asian tiger mosquito is native to Asia. It made its way to the United States in the 1980s. The mosquitos arrived on boats full of used tires. These bugs breed in pools of water. You guessed it—the old tires were perfect pools for laying eggs. As they traveled across the ocean, more and more mosquitos were born. When the containers of tires were opened, the bugs flew out.

This mosquito has a nasty bite. For twenty years, towns on the East Coast have fought off the tiger mosquito species. To stop the bug from spreading, they got rid of all standing water. They also sprayed chemicals. Tires were inspected, too, and the bug stayed controlled in the East. All the efforts worked fairly well, for a while.

In 2001, workers on the West Coast opened up containers filled with shoots of "lucky bamboo." This is a popular plant to give to friends and family. The green shoots were stacked in large, open pools of water. Can you guess what happened next? Out flew Asian tiger mosquitos! The West Coast version of the mosquito invasion had begun. Today, this biting bug can be found across the United States.

We try to quickly control alien insect outbreaks where we can. We spray chemicals, make new laws, and go out in teams to find them. Whole towns and states make action plans to control the bugs. However, humans are still capable of costly errors. These mistakes can set insects on a path to destruction.

Crops and Goods

Some invasive insects don't just hurt people. They hurt our food sources and survival. European corn borers were first brought into the United States from Italy and Hungary in the early 1900s. Today, they can be found all across the country. You can find them crawling inside many types of crops. They create infestations, in which a plant is totally overrun by another living thing. Corn borers can plague several types of corn, beans, wheat, and peppers. This can completely ruin fields of plants that should be food. Over the last several decades, scientists and farmers have found some ways

NOW STARRING ... BUGS!

Over the years, insects have played a starring role in hundreds of science fiction and horror movies. Hollywood loves bugs! These characters are true invaders, attacking cities, animals, and people on a large scale. *Swarm*, which premiered in the 1970s, tells the story of a killer bee invasion in Texas. These bees attack helicopters, swarm a nuclear power plant, and take down an entire town!

Of course, these movies are popular because of how crazy they are. "Killer" bees could never do such damage. Movies like these show just how troubled we are about invasive insects. They also show how powerful our imaginations can be. Terrifying invasive species including bees, flies, ants, beetles, grasshoppers, and more have appeared in films. You can now find hundreds of sci-fi and scary movies featuring insect invaders.

to deal with the corn borer. They have tried chemical sprays, light traps, and the use of natural enemies. One of these enemies is the ladybird beetle. Farmers can buy ladybugs and release them on their fields. Unlike some other invasive insects, the European corn borer doesn't bite humans or give us diseases. However,

A BIG STINK

One invasive bug poses a serious threat ... to our noses! The brown marmorated stink bug was discovered in Pennsylvania in 1998. This insect invites itself into homes in the fall. It is always looking for a winter hideout. The shield-shaped bug creeps into houses and sleeps. It doesn't sting or bite, but it does stink. When it feels scared, the BMSB lets out a strong, gross odor. Some people are even allergic to the smell. These bugs now live in several states. The only way to stop stink bugs is to keep them out. Left outside in the winter, they freeze.

their continued spread can have serious effects on the food supply for animals and people.

As we've seen, many insects have been moved by accident, through old tires or **untreated wood**. Others are invited into a new host country on purpose. Remember the gypsy moth that has been eating through American forests? It first entered the United States when a man from France, Leopold Trouvelot, wanted to start a silk business. Silk comes from silk worms, which grow into moths. Silk worms, however, are delicate and hard to raise, so Leopold tried to breed silk moths and gypsy moths together. The gypsy moth is easy to raise because it tends to eat everything in sight! After a few months, Trouvelot accidentally let some of the gypsy moths out of his backyard. He started an invasion that hasn't stopped since. Trouvelot reported the outbreak, but he soon returned to France, and the rest is history.

Boll Weevil

Scientific Name: *Anthonomus grandis*

Looks Like: Grey-black beetle with a long snout, usually around 0.25 inches (6 millimeters) long

Eats: Flowers and buds of the cotton plant

Origin: Mexico

Moved To: United States

Year of Move: 1892

Cause: Unknown

Impact: The boll weevil entered the United States at the wrong time. In 1892, most southern farmers sold cotton. They needed the plant to survive! The weevil ate cotton … and more cotton. The crops were ruined. This caused chaos during the early 1900s. Many farmers lost jobs and money. It nearly ended the US cotton industry.

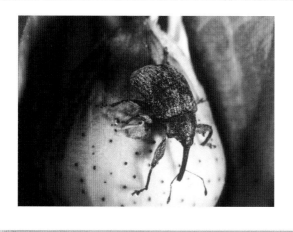

Spread: The **United States Department of Agriculture (USDA)** is still working to stamp out the boll weevil in states that grow cotton. This has worked in many states, like Georgia, Florida, and the Carolinas. The effort is still underway in many others.

Note: The harm of some invasive insects is hard to forget. Over the years, a few of these bugs have become famous. The boll weevil was a popular subject of poems and blues songs during the Great Depression. There is now a boll weevil statue in Alabama. The University of Arkansas even uses the boll weevil as its mascot. You can see the big green bug on the court at basketball games and other events. The people of the South will never forget this cotton-eating insect!

Mediterranean Fruit Fly (Medfly)

Scientific Name: *Ceratitis capitata*

Looks Like: Tiny fruit fly with black and yellow markings and clear wings. These flies have a unique look. They are easy to tell apart from other types.

Eats: Medflies eat more than 260 different nuts, fruits, vegetables, and flowers. Some of their favorites are mangos, figs, peaches, and plums.

Origin: Sub-Saharan Africa

Moved To: South and Central America, Australia, the Mediterranean region, the Middle East, and Hawaii

Year of Move: Spread began in the 1880s

Cause: Trading fruits, flowers, and vegetables between countries

Impact: Medflies thrive in fruits with thin skins. Their travel across the globe has allowed them to make homes in new types of plants. They now invade

coffee, avocados, papayas, and more. They are very damaging to crops.

Spread: The medfly is now found all across the Earth. It has not become a problem on the US mainland. The United States has taken serious efforts to control and stop its spread. It was first brought to Hawaii in 1907 and has since stayed there.

Africanized Honeybee (AHB)

Scientific name: The western honeybee is known as *Apis mellifera*. The "Africanized" honeybee is *Apis mellifera scutellata*.

Looks Like: The AHB looks just like the European or "western" bee, the kind typically seen in the United States. The African and Africanized bees are slightly smaller, but you have to use a **microscope** to spot the difference!

Origin: African honeybees are native to Africa. The other honeybees found in the United States are from Europe. This means that *all* of the honeybees in America are invasive species! The European bees, however, have been in North America for much longer. When African bees mate with European bees, the African traits win out, creating the AHB.

Move: Honeybees were first brought to North America from Europe in the 1600s. African bees weren't brought into South America until the late 1950s, by a scientist named Dr. Warwick Kerr. He wanted to do tests on them. The bees quickly spread through Central and South America. They mated with European bees and created the hybrid AHB. They entered the United States in 1990.

Impact: Both honeybees have been great for the United States—except for the stings, of course. Bees are important for farming. The AHB helps with **pollination,** the process that allows plants to make seeds. It also produces honey, just like the western species. Unfortunately, the Africanized species is easily angered. European honeybees are calm and docile, but AHBs will defend their nests in large groups. They usually fly very fast. You may also know the AHB by its nickname, the "killer bee." Don't be misled, though, because its sting isn't any more harmful than the sting of European bees.

Spread: The AHB is slowly spreading throughout the United States It now covers a range of states from California to Florida. Its growth is limited by the climate. The AHB demands warmer climates in order to live and reproduce. You should not expect to see these "killer bees" north of Utah anytime soon.

People in communities all across America are working together to stop the spread of invasive insects and diseases. This parks commissioner in Forest Park, Queens, is taking a look at a log filled with holes from the Asian longhorned beetle.

Aliens Are Everywhere

No matter where you live on our planet, you are likely to meet invasive insects. Whether you are in a forest, on a boat, or even in your own house, there are probably aliens nearby. Some of these bugs have painful bites, such as fire ants, or cause terrible damage to buildings, like termites. Others fit in with their habitat, like Africanized bees. They help create honey and look just like the native bees.

When it comes to these invaders, there are a few things that people can do to help control their spread and harm. Kids can help, too! Teams of regular adults and children in Massachusetts have been trained to spot signs of the Asian longhorned beetle. This beetle

AVOIDANCE IS THE BEST POLICY

Some invasive insects have spread so far, and have such potential for harm, that the best thing you can do is avoid them. When it comes to bugs like the Asian tiger mosquito, which might carry disease, be sure to apply insect repellant. Wear long sleeves and pants when outdoors for long periods of time. If you think you might be sick, tell your parent or doctor. For swarms of bees of any type, not just Africanized bees, professionals suggest that you do nothing more than "bee aware" and listen, look, and run. Sometimes, just keeping your eyes and ears open is the best way to deal with invasive species.

Always wear long pants, sleeves, socks, and boots when taking a hike in the woods. You never know where mosquitoes, ticks, and other bugs might be lurking!

has been eating up Massachusetts's beautiful forests for years, and local people want it wiped out. Groups go on walks in the woods and mark trees that might be infested. Later, they work hard to replant the trees that have been cut down. These citizens are slowly rebuilding the forests they love so much.

There are also websites to visit and numbers to call when you think you've spotted an insect like the ALB, gypsy moth, or others. Look for some examples in the "Find Out More" section of this book. State governments and the USDA keep track of these species very carefully. Some insects can be wiped out. For others, the best we can do is to manage their numbers. If we want to stop the spread of invasive bugs, it is up to us to be aware of the species living around us. We should also learn about the creatures that could soon move into our neighborhoods, fields, and parks.

Common types of control include spraying or burying chemicals and setting traps. In some areas, infected crops and plants are cut down, or even burned. Many invasive bugs affect crops like fruits, corn, and cotton. Taking our food back from these species is hard work, but some efforts are on track.

The boll weevil has been removed from most of the American South. The USDA is starting programs to slow their spread in our forests. For many years now, laws have been in place that try to oversee international trade, particularly the exchange of plants and animals between countries. This may slow or stop the flow of invasive species. Unfortunately, as we've seen, these measures don't always work. In our lifetimes, we will probably see even more invasive insects move from place to place, some helping and many more harming our environment.

Chemical sprays are one form of invasive insect and disease control. However, we don't yet know how these chemicals will affect our planet in the long term.

GLOSSARY

adaptation A trait that an organism develops and maintains in order to better survive and multiply in an environment.

antennae A pair of long, sensitive organs on the head of an insect.

defoliation The act of destroying or causing the loss of leaves.

food chain A series of connections between living things, starting with plants, which produce their own energy, and moving on to animals, which get energy by eating plants or other animals.

global trade The system of buying and selling that occurs between different countries across the world.

habitat The place where a living thing, like a plant or animal, lives.

infestation A state in which a habitat or organism is overrun by another living thing.

microscope A tool used for viewing very small objects.

organism An individual living thing. Plants, animals, and fungi are all organisms.

overpopulation When there are too many organisms for the number of resources in an area.

pollination The transfer of pollen between flowering plants, which allows those plants to make seeds and reproduce.

predator Any animal that eats other animals.

prey Any animal that is hunted by humans or other animals for food.

United States Department of Agriculture (USDA)
A federal organization that makes policies on farming, forestry, and food.

untreated wood Natural lumber that has not been infused with chemicals.

FIND OUT MORE

Books

Albee, Sarah. *Bugged: How Insects Changed History*. New York: Walker Books for Young Readers, 2014.

Burns, Loree Griffin. *Beetle Busters: A Rogue Insect and the People Who Track It*. Scientists in the Field. Boston, MA: HMH Books for Young Readers, 2014.

Murawski, Darlyne and Nancy Honovich. *Ultimate Bugopedia: The Most Complete Bug Reference Ever*. National Geographic Kids. Washington, DC: National Geographic Children's Books, 2013.

Shaw, Gina. *The Buzz on Insects*. New York: Penguin Young Readers, 2016.

Websites

Asian Longhorned Beetle
www.asianlonghornedbeetle.com
This site, supported by the USDA, promotes the identification and capture of the ALB. If you want to help the

efforts underway in your state, or if you think you've spotted signs of the ALB, you can report your findings here!

Don't Move Firewood

www.dontmovefirewood.org

This website, developed by the Continental Dialogue on Non-Native Forest Insects and Diseases, aims to educate about common invasive pests living in forests and highlights the ways in which people can help.

National Environmental Coalition on Invasive Species

www.necis.net

The NECIS promotes policies and educates the public on invasive species. It includes both basic information and news items.

National Wildlife Federation

www.nwf.org

The NWF offers up-to-date information about animals and habitats affected by invasive species.

INDEX

Page numbers in **boldface** are illustrations. Entries in **boldface** are glossary terms.

ABOUT THE AUTHOR

Kaitlyn Duling grew up in the Midwest, where invasive beetles and corn borers were definitely a problem! She has worked at both a veterinary clinic and a livestock farm but now enjoys working on a bookmobile, writing grants for a children's education nonprofit, and helping kids (just like you!) learn to love reading. Today, she resides in Pittsburgh, Pennsylvania, where she is forever finding brown marmorated stink bugs in her apartment.